PIANO • VOCAL • GUITAR

CHRIS TOMLIN
AND IF OUR GOD IS FOR US...

Original Album Design by Jesse Owen

ISBN 978-1-61774-091-6

7777 W. BLUEMOUND RD. P.O. BOX 13819 MILWAUKEE, WI 53213

Visit Hal Leonard Online at
www.halleonard.com

Our God

Words and Music by
CHRIS TOMLIN, JESSE REEVES,
MATT REDMAN, and JONAS MYRIN

Chords Used in This Song

I Will Follow

Words and Music by
CHRIS TOMLIN, REUBEN MORGAN,
and JASON INGRAM

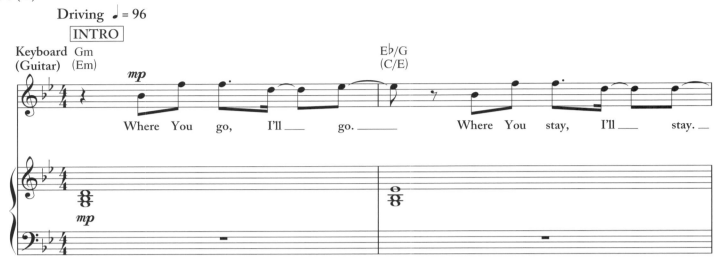

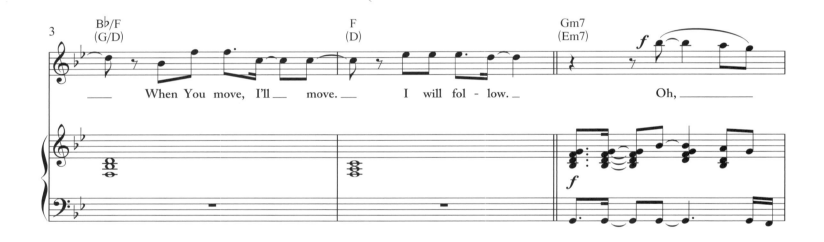

11

12

CHORUS

joy, — and I will fol - low. — Where You go, I'll — go. —

Where You stay, I'll — stay. — When You move, I'll — move. —

I will fol - low. — Who You love, I'll — love. —

How You serve, I'll — serve. — If this life I — lose, — I will fol - low. —

Chords Used in This Song

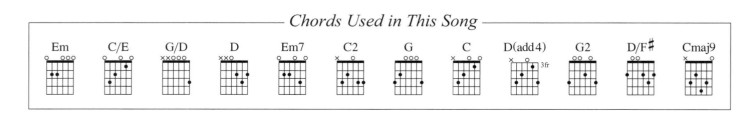

I Lift My Hands

Words and Music by
CHRIS TOMLIN, LOUIE GIGLIO,
and MATT MAHER

Capo 3 (G)

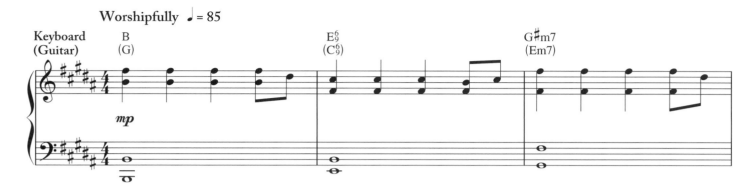

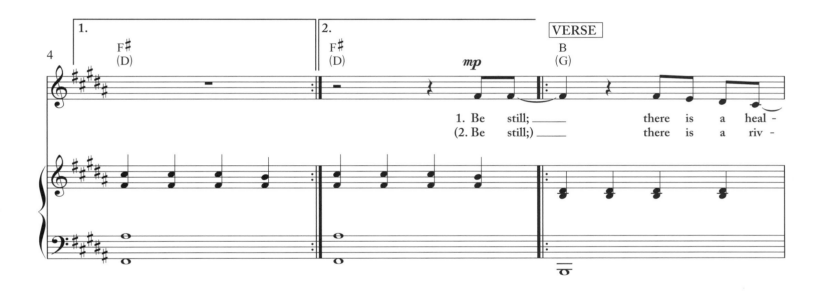

1. Be still; _____ there is a heal-
(2. Be still;) _____ there is a riv-

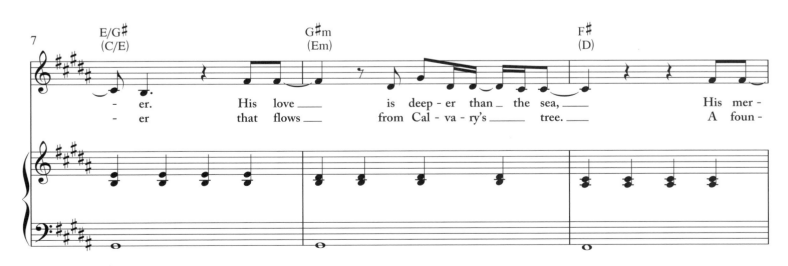

-er. His love _____ is deep-er than _ the sea, _____ His mer-
-er that flows _____ from Cal-va-ry's _____ tree. _____ A foun-

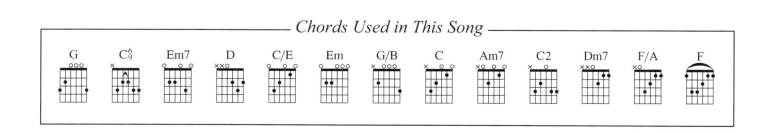

Chords Used in This Song

Majesty of Heaven

Words and Music by
CHRIS TOMLIN, JESSE REEVES,
and MATT REDMAN

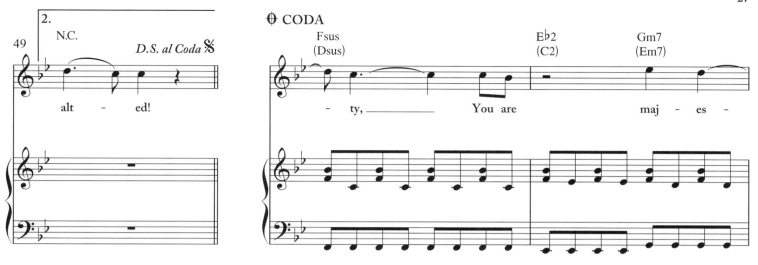

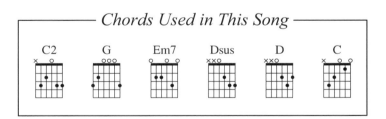

No Chains on Me

Words and Music by
CHRIS TOMLIN, JESSE REEVES,
and MATT REDMAN

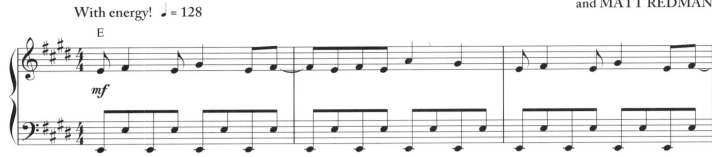

Chords Used in This Song

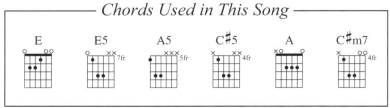

Lovely

Words and Music by
CHRIS TOMLIN and JASON INGRAM

Moderately ♩ = 80

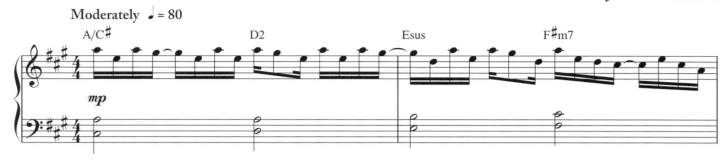

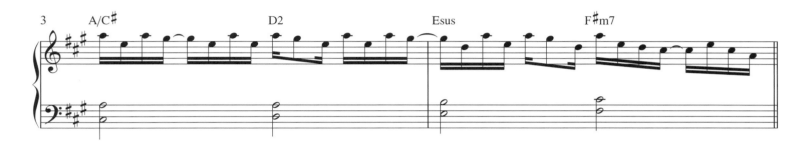

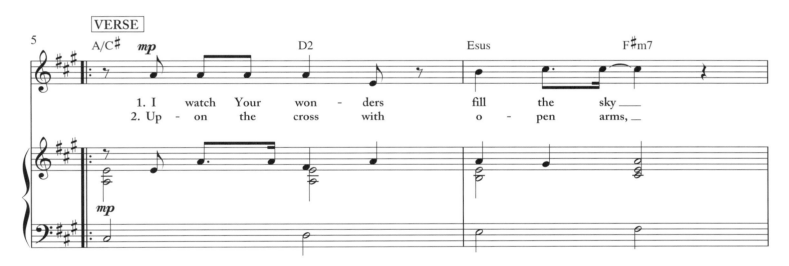

VERSE

1. I watch Your won-ders fill the sky ___
2. Up-on the cross with o-pen arms, ___

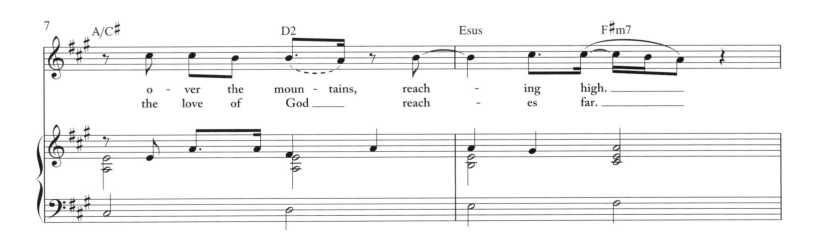

o - ver the moun - tains, reach - ing high. ___
the love of God ___ reach - es far. ___

wor - thy of. ___

You _ are wor-

- thy. _____

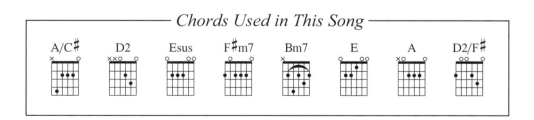

Chords Used in This Song

A/C♯ D2 Esus F♯m7 Bm7 E A D2/F♯

The Name of Jesus

Words and Music by
CHRIS TOMLIN, JESSE REEVES,
MATT REDMAN, DANIEL CARSON,
KRISTIAN STANFILL, and ED CASH

Capo 3 (C)

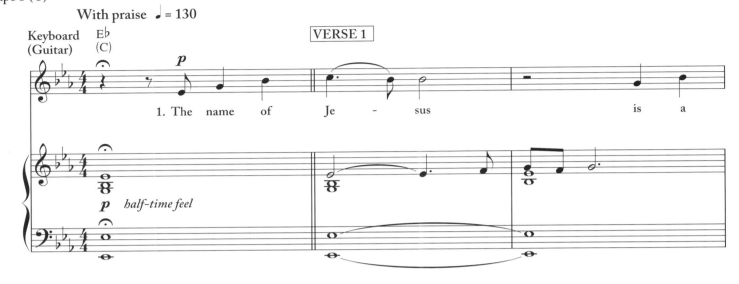

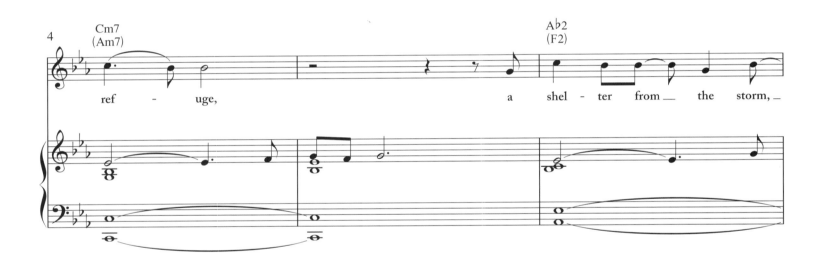

44

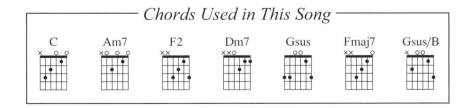

All to Us

Words and Music by
CHRIS TOMLIN, JESSE REEVES,
MATT REDMAN, and MATT MAHER

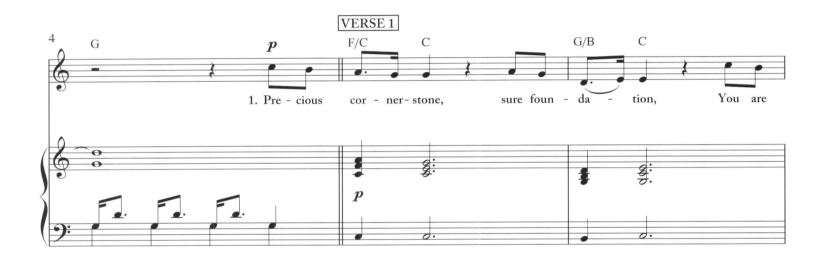

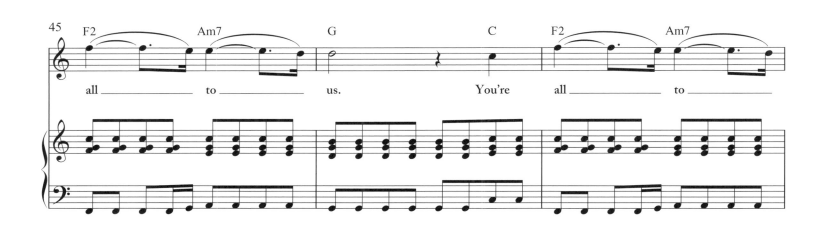

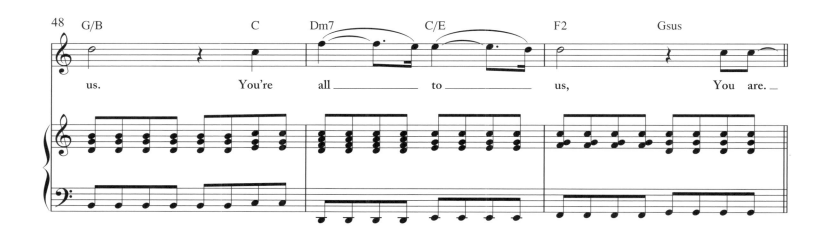

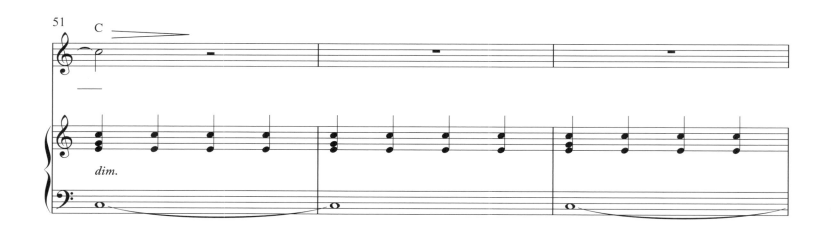

VERSE 3

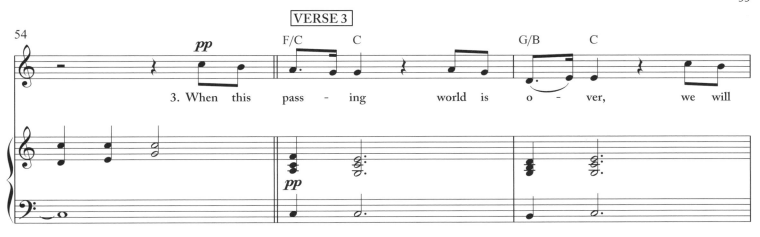

3. When this pass - ing world is o - ver, we will

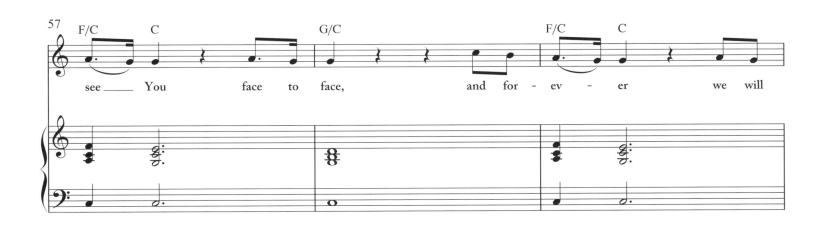

see ___ You face to face, and for - ev - er we will

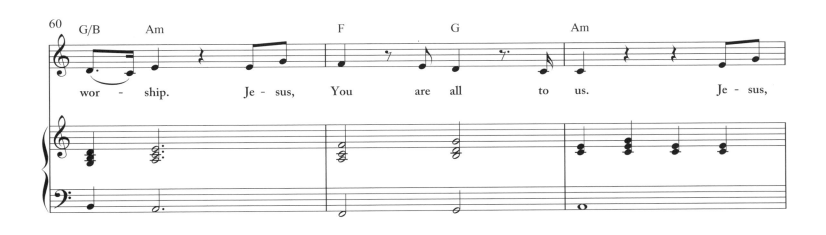

wor - ship. Je - sus, You are all to us. Je - sus,

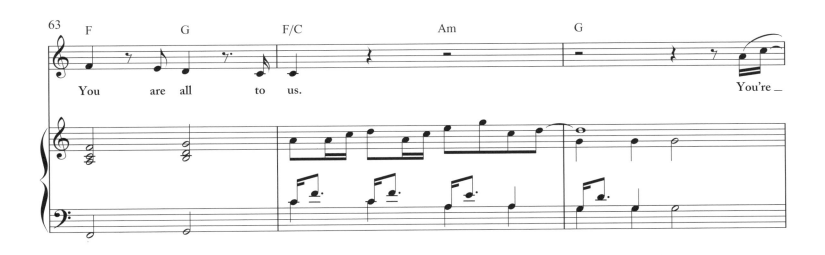

You are all to us. You're ___

56

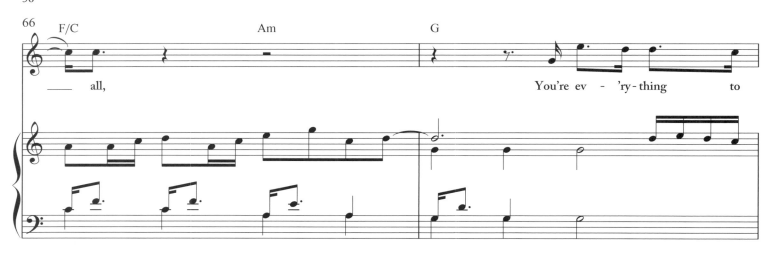

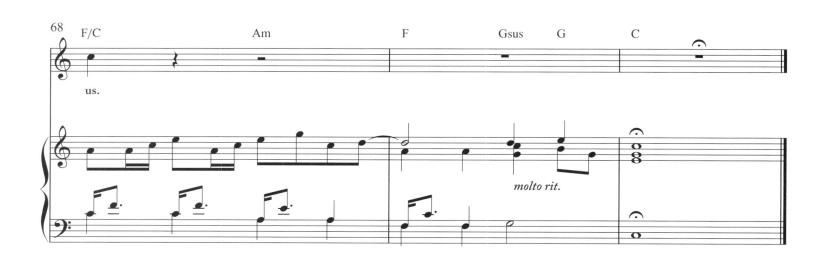

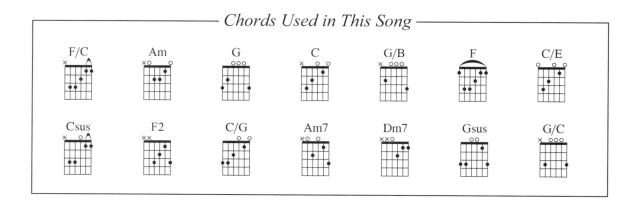

Chords Used in This Song

Faithful

Words and Music by
CHRIS TOMLIN, CHRISTY NOCKELS,
NATHAN NOCKELS, and ED CASH

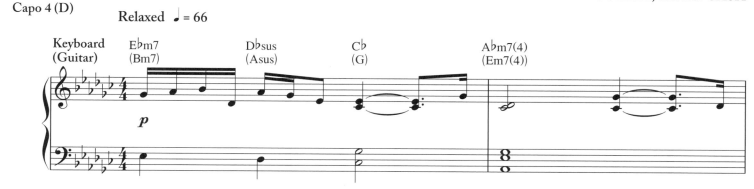

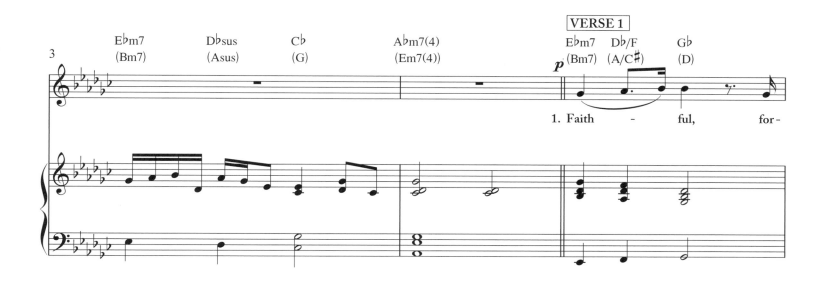

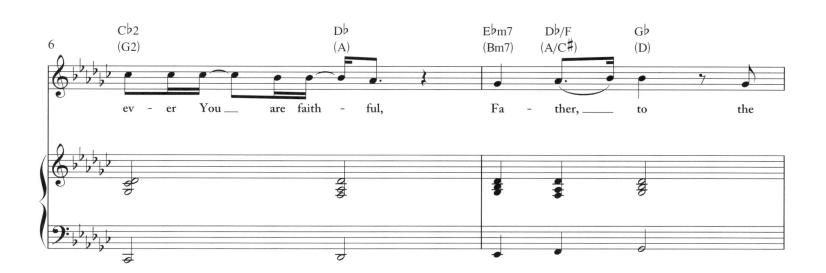

in ev - 'ry seas - on.   You are there,
seas - on of __ my soul. __   You are there, _____   You're the

You're the an - chor.   You are there   in the
an - chor that __ will __ hold.   You are there _____   in the

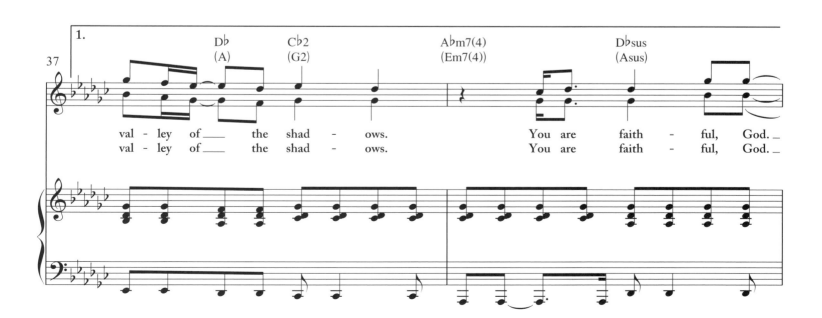

val - ley of __ the shad - ows.   You are faith - ful, God. __
val - ley of __ the shad - ows.   You are faith - ful, God. __

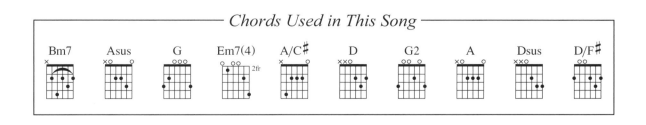

Chords Used in This Song

Jesus, My Redeemer

Words and Music by
CHRIS TOMLIN, DANIEL CARSON,
and JASON INGRAM

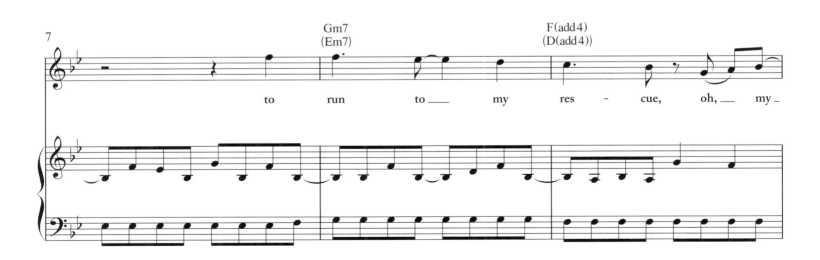

66

68

BRIDGE

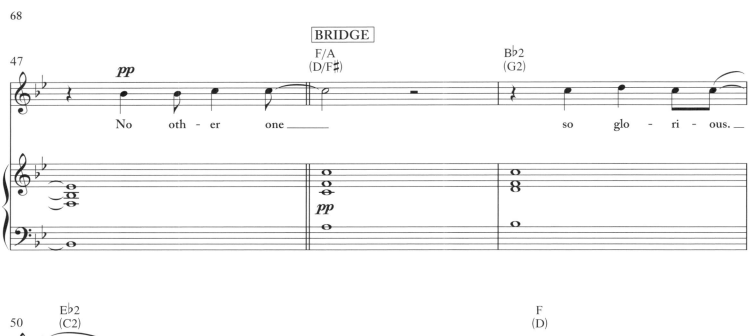

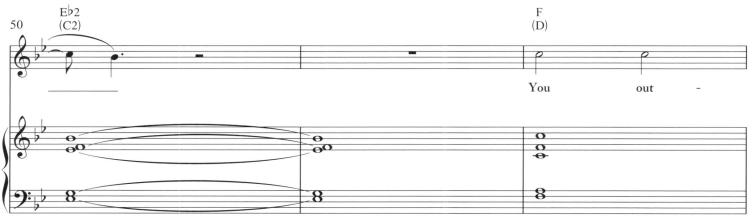

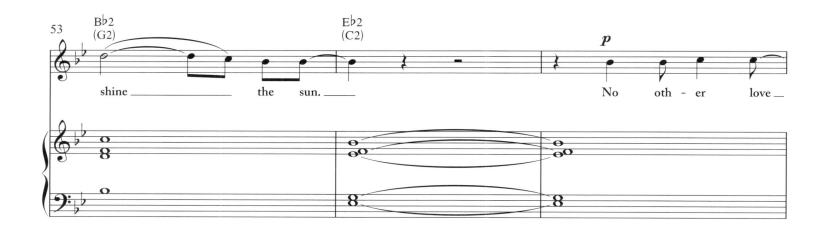

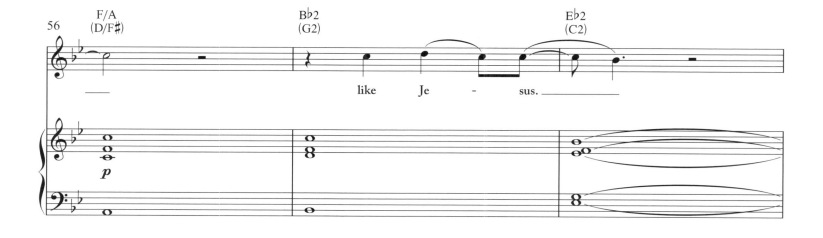

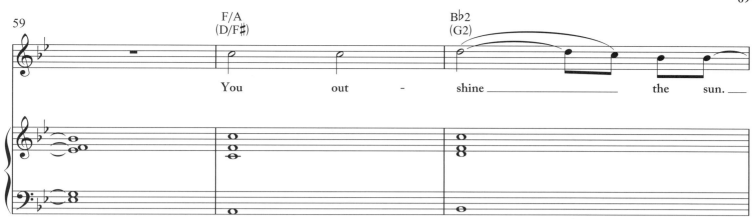

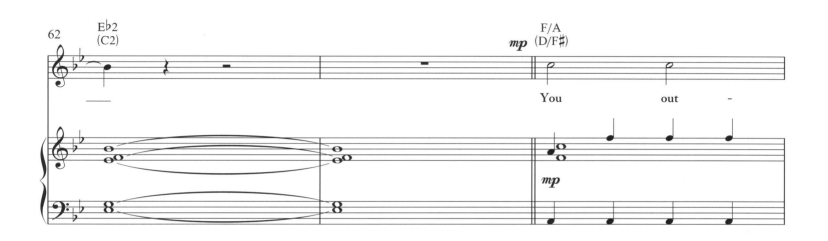

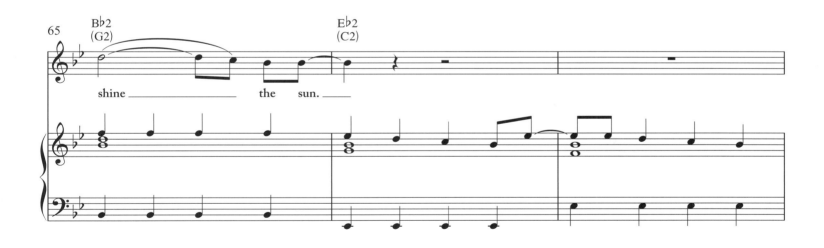

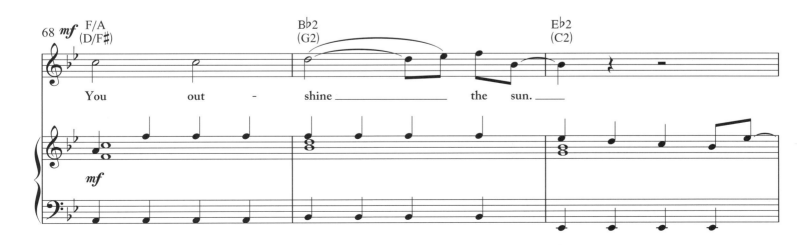

CHORUS

And oh, __ You shine! _____ How __ You shine! __

My __ Re - deem - er.

slight rit.

Chords Used in This Song

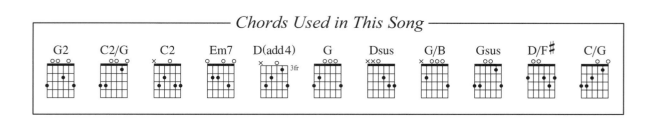

G2   C2/G   C2   Em7   D(add 4)   G   Dsus   G/B   Gsus   D/F#   C/G

Awakening

Words and Music by
REUBEN MORGAN
and CHRIS TOMLIN

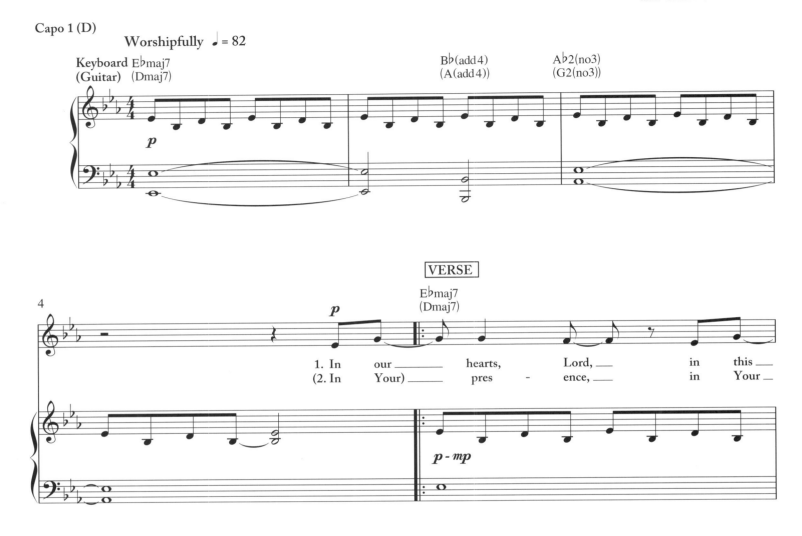

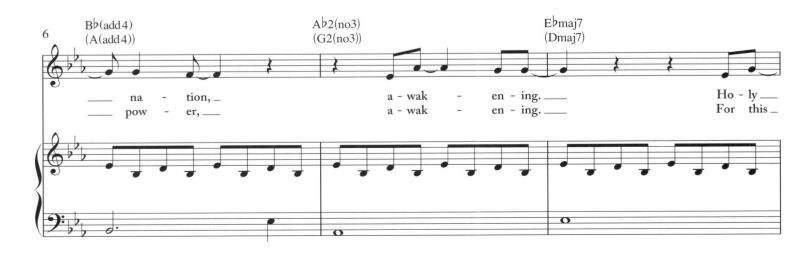

75

80

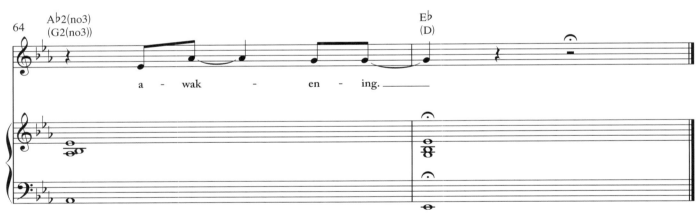

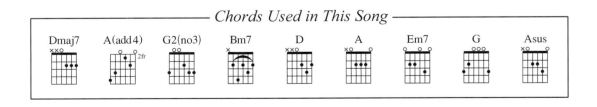

Chords Used in This Song